Etruscan Things

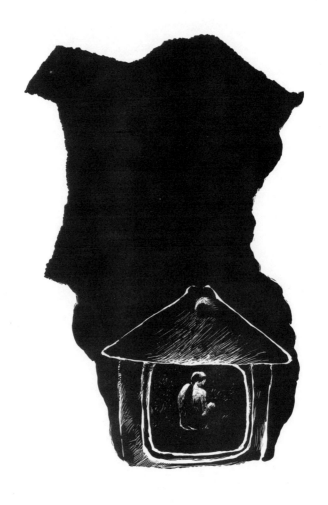

Etruscan Things

poems by RIKA LESSER

with a note by Richard Howard

Illustrations by Paul O. Zelinsky

GEORGE BRAZILLER · NEW YORK

12/1983
gen'l

Some of the poems in this volume originally appeared in the following periodicals (some in slightly different form):

THE AMERICAN POETRY REVIEW: *Guardiana Della Sepoltura, Canopic Jar, Vortex, From Vetulonia, The Mummy Speaks, La Defunta, Hut Urn, Calchas, Haruspex, La Banditaccia, 1979*
THE KENYON REVIEW: *The Warning*
THE MASSACHUSETTS REVIEW: *Lucien's Ploughman 1848*
THE NEW REPUBLIC: *Sarcophagus*
PRAIRIE SCHOONER: *A Handle on Things*
SHENANDOAH: *Hand to Hand*

Published in the United States in 1983 by George Braziller, Inc.
Copyright 1979, 1980, 1981, 1982, 1983 by Rika Lesser. All rights reserved.
Illustrations Copyright 1983 by Paul O. Zelinsky

Grateful acknowledgement is made to the following for permission to reprint:
Excerpt from ETRUSCAN PLACES by D. H. Lawrence. Originally published by the Viking Press, Inc. in 1932. Reprinted by permission of Viking Penguin Inc. All rights reserved.
Excerpt from DUINESER ELEGIEN by Rainer Maria Rilke. Copyright 1923 Insel Verlag, Frankfurt.
Excerpt from THE INTERPRETATION OF DREAMS by Sigmund Freud, translated from the German and edited by James Strachey, published in the United States by Basic Books, Inc., Publishers, New York by arrangement with George Allen & Unwin Ltd. and The Hogarth Press, Ltd., London.

For information address the publisher:
George Braziller, Inc.
One Park Avenue
New York, NY 10016

Library of Congress Cataloging in Publication Data
Lesser, Rika. *Etruscan things.*
(The Braziller series of poetry) 1. Etruscans—Poetry. I. Title.
PS3562.E837E8   1983   811.54   82-12824
ISBN 0-8076-1058-5
ISBN 0-8076-1059-3 (pbk.)

Printed in the United States of America.   ·   First Edition

Designed by Renée Cossutta

for my mother and father

Contents

Acknowledgments

I BECAME INTERESTED in Etruscan things almost inadvertently, in October 1977, while revising translations of two poems in Gunnar Ekelöf's *Guide to the Underworld*. Ingrid Ekelöf, the poet's widow, wrote me that Gunnar was referring to some Etruscan wall paintings. About the Etruscans I knew nothing, and immediately I walked into a second-hand bookshop, emerging with a general book on Etruscan and early Roman art. The text was stuffy but the plates were excellent. One of them started speaking to or, rather, through me, and has been converted into the poem "Canopic Jar." Not long afterwards, Richard Howard gave me his Everyman's Library edition of George Dennis. I would never have begun or continued these poems without the enthusiasm and support of Ingrid Ekelöf and Richard Howard, nor without the guidance of Gunnar Ekelöf's spirit, which breathed life into a number of the poems. My deepest debt of gratitude is to these three.

Of all the books on the Etruscans, the ones I love best are George Dennis's two-volume *The Cities and Cemeteries of Etruria* (1848), D. H. Lawrence's *Etruscan Places* (1932), and for its comprehensive collection of illustrations, G. Q. Giglioli's *L'Arte Etrusca* (Milan, 1935).

I want to thank the Ingram Merrill Foundation for a grant to work on these poems; it got me out of the libraries and into Etruria proper in 1979.

Many other friends and acquaintances have given spiritual or factual guidance, but I shall name only half a dozen. Warm thanks go to Simone Golby for helping me translate Lucien Bonaparte's lines; to Judith Hoberman and Dominic Kinsley for lending me their library cards and sometimes transporting heavy tomes between New Haven and New York; to

Anne-Marie Nielsen of the Ny Carlsberg Glyptotek in Copenhagen, for resolving the question of which was the head- and which the foot-end of a sarcophagus in that museum, described divergently in two catalogues; to Ernesto Macchiaiolo of the Museo Nazionale Etrusco in Chiusi, for temporarily bestowing upon me the title of *"professoressa,"* so that I could visit the Tomb of the Monkey without the necessary papers; and to Paul O. Zelinsky for preventing the notes to this book from becoming all too Kinbotean an affair.

Rika Lesser

A Note on Rika Lesser

We touch, we hold, we keep / one another free

IT IS THE IMPERATIVE, as well as the privilege, of all such through-composed works as *Etruscan Things*—of all those covens and clutches of poems confederated to arrive at a structure, a meaning from contiguity, contrast and recurrence, rather than disposed to afford the pleasures of merely circulating among separate feats, discretions—that we *have read* the entire production before we linger over, before we pluck out any one member of the concatenation, any particular limb of the body. We date our modernity, almost, from such affairs as *Leaves of Grass*, as *Fleurs du Mal*, whose "secret architecture," as Baudelaire called it, articulates a vision beyond the anthologist's dream. Rika Lesser has learned, translating Rilke, translating Ekelöf, the likelihood such structures have of resisting not only the intelligence but oblivion as well, of sticking to the mind because they make a shape in the memory. She has gone to some trouble to devise a scheme of this kind, a map of earthly ruins which corresponds, it would seem, to that map of the skies by which a repressed culture once secured its wisdom and its joy. Nothing appears less *actual*, of course, than the question of the Etruscans (who were to the Romans what the Jews were to the Germans, and to the Romans as well, according to Tacitus) and their sky maps, their divination from the courses of lightning through the starry sky, until we realize that we bear, still, within our language, vestiges of this practice. Each time we *consider*, each time we *contemplate*, we make a sidereal temple of the stars, setting them in significant order, a constellation. So I would suggest that the first way of dealing with this new guide to the ruins is to read it through, notes and all, without stopping over bright particular beauties, though there are plenty of them, and even without trying to "figure out" what the "intellectual" intentions of left and right, near and far, intimate and hostile, might be. It is my experience with these poems that their tephromancy—their divination by ashes—can be trusted, and that by the time you come round to the celebrated couple in the twenty-fourth poem, the *sposi:*

> Sharing the single bed, how close
> we lie; fingers curved over palms
> whose fable reads: *conjugal bliss*
> *is possible.*

—you will feel that you have experienced—suffered, recovered, enjoyed—a version of vision which, perhaps for being so fragmentary, so supputative, is the more *telling*, the more striking for being stricken.

Cunning and compassionate, resourceful and responsive Rika Lesser has been (perhaps they are the same thing —not a thing at all but a mode of *taking in*, whereby the poet is made merely a vessel, a means of rendering justice to the visible world which, thus pronounced, replies in *sentences:* ". . . transformed the words. They entered my flesh, / became whole inside me. Black ink on / white cloth: opaque remains. The meanings / lie in the lacunae")—so submissive to the evidence that I am at a loss, and happy to be there, whether what I am calling the presented vision of a whole culture, a society, a way of being human, proceeds more vividly from her recuperation of the Etruscan things themselves, or from their wreck: is it the story of loss and ruin which tells us more, the evidence of destruction, than any restored emblem ("reconstructed from about 400 fragments") might dissert?

In either case, or in the accumulated pressure of both at once, the Etruscan *gestus* and the text of fragmentation, these poems contest the primacy placed by most of us, most of the time, on a life defined by reason, utility and discursive order. Here the attention is bestowed upon those practices and attitudes which acknowledge death as a force of life rather than its tragic demise. Solitude, isolation and despair are—however momentarily—overcome within ecstatic instants, apprehensions of continuity labeled sacred in "archaic" cultures. These are poems which rehearse the affirmative willingness to lose things, meanings, and even the self (the self most of all, for if the self is the God in everyone, it cannot be fully entered into). Rika Lesser has determined upon the intuition of ruins secretly awaited, where the sustained value is intensity, a concentration of energy antithetical to the husbanding of scarce resources, disdainful of immediate ends, resolved upon the transgressive violence of sacrifice, a rite where paradoxically the moment of eroticism transcends sexuality (eroticism being to sexuality as the nondiscursive is to language). As we see in the final poem, to look at a person laughing—it is the subversive insight of Georges Bataille which I borrow here—can be a form of erotic encounter.

These conclusions or reductions cannot, evidently, be warranted by any one poem, or even by the eminently quotable and cunningly enjambed movements within any one poem, though I find these lines irresistible as a liminary invitation (and admonition):

> Nothing our own hands fashion
> endures intact. Weather will
> have its way, eating into
> these faces, making queer shapes
> of our work. And some future
> race will worry these contours,
> forcing open its false doors.
> None but the Hand of Sky—palm
> blazoned with thunderbolts, streaked
> with burning stars—on the day
> it clasps the Hand of Earth
> (crushing our bones to powder)
> can bring the temple down.

One is obliged to read *Etruscan Things* in the way Eliot suggested we read *Anabasis*—by yielding to its serial pressure, letting the stubborn center be scattered where the poet, in her will-to-vanishings, intends her artifice to be undone. Then we discover the dire, fastidious significance of Rika Lesser's poems, which are of course a meditation on what happens to the open secret of her life, what becomes of *now*; we discover, in so many Etruscan things taken out of their Etruscan places, that the past pollutes AND saves.

Richard Howard

Pars Dextra (Hostilis)

In matters of such antiquity,
I hold it sufficient if what
seemeth truth be received as such.

Livy

A Handle on Things

Molded into a shape the hand
wants to hold,
the smooth bronze of a body
in miniature:

My head rests on the blade,
hair and neck stiff, arms bent
back and raised, my body, a girl's
body lets you use an incense shovel.

Stout warriors, we twin brothers
gaze past our beards, bear
his weight on opposite arms:
Our spears cannot prod him
to life. May Charun not raise
his hammer above this youth's
fair head.

Broken off from our objects
we wrestle, offer
libations, perform
acrobatics, blow the curved
horn, dance with satyrs, embrace
one another's shoulders.
Embrace as Tages ordered
when he gave the Law to Tarchon.

Touch us. Hold us. Keep us.
What we were attached to
lost long ago.

Lucien's Ploughman   1848

That small bronze model found up north, near Arezzo,
embodies my daily rounds of twenty years past,
though its own age is twenty-one centuries.
The little ploughman, a wide-brimmed cap on his head,
leans backward, digs his heels into the earth;
his fingers barely graze the swing-plough's long
handle. His heavy-shouldered oxen are placid
under the yoke. A light, firm touch guides them.
Today we have better tools—no better masters.
We are the beasts of burden, the human ploughs.

My leg aches—every time it rains;
An old break, from the day we fell through to God
knows what infernal depth. My former master,
Monsieur Lucien Bonaparte, *il principe
di Canino*, was off gazing at stars when it
happened. Had he been here—at Vulci—I like
to think he'd have had us cast in bronze, added
to his collection, *Museum Etrusque*:

> "In the beginning of the year
> eighteen hundred twenty-eight,
> in a field called CAVALUPO,
> the ground gave way, turned
> grotto beneath the hooves
> of oxen dragging a plough."

Who ever heard of oxen doing anything
unattended? It was I who drove them close by
the castle wall. A medieval fortress, guarded
now by the Pope's *doganieri*, Bonaparte's

castle stands on the verge of a steep cliff. Down
below, the Fiora frets, deepens its channel.
A bridge spans the gulf, a narrow bridge with high
parapets, slung with stalactites: a beard of
icicles, long and yellowish-white. We dared not
cross the Ponte della Badia; avoiding
the ravine, we ploughed tableland.

> "Found in this grotto were two
> broken Etruscan vases."

They broke under our weight but did not shatter.
The fired clay proved less fragile than the ground,
my bones, or the necks of the oxen.

> "I was absent from my lands
> for over a year: two
> perfidious agents took
> the vases, dug many months
> in secret, searching for more . . ."

Bless them, they heard my cries and pulled me out
(with the vases) of the dark stone hole that rang
with the last deep bellow of my team. A dungeon
I thought—Lord knows I'd have rotted there until
I matched the bones and ashes in those urns. But I
was fortunate, even in my fall. Five years
before, in Corneto-Tarquinia, digging
for stones to mend a road, Carlo Avvolta
unearthed a *nenfro* slab, made a hole beneath it,
saw a man in full armor on a stone bier.
In his right hand a sword, a lance and javelins
on the bench. When air met flesh the body heaved,
trembled, shook, crumbled to powder (as we all will).
The delicate gold crown Avvolta lifted
out of the tomb dissolved en route to Rome. Thank God
I landed not in a warrior's but a common grave.

> "Furtively they sold all the vases
> to a Monsieur Dorow, who himself
> several times returned to Canino,
> doubtless believing the true owners
> to be aware of his undertakings. . . ."

Having sold the vases, Dorow, I believe, paid
off the Prince, but did not, I gather, reap as vast
a return on the graveyard goods as Lucien who'd
bought the unhallowed, hollow lands from the Pope.
When he returned *il principe* had my saviors flogged.

> "In the month of October the Princess
> ordered excavations begun . . .
> near the Ponte della Badia,
> banking on the Fiora. The first
> attempts produced only a few
> vases, but the quality of several
> fragments sufficed to encourage
> the Princess to continue the work
> with a constancy to which we owe
> all our discoveries."

The bridge I've described, but what of the Princess?
These eight years she has outlived her husband.
The widow Jouberthou, for twenty years of
excavations the envy of all Europe,
not for her constancy, but the ornaments
she wears: gold, amber, ivory necklaces and rings
removed from the graves of superior women.
Evviva la principessa! To her we owe
the annual displeasure of digging up
our hectares, searching each winter for buried
treasure the plains we plough and sow with wheat each spring.
Below the topsoil the earth is friable
tufa, caves in on the contents of underworld
chambers no man has the right to unseal.
But we must dig meticulously, sift out
every shard, each splinter, every glimmer
of a gem. Should we find larger objects:
coarse clay fired black, incised, unvarnished ware,
though nicely turned, these we must dash to the ground,
learn to call them *"roba di sciocchezza,"* foolish
stuff, crush them under our bootsoles, so that higher
prices prevail on the market. High above us
the *capo* sits clutching his gun, a constant
reminder of my saviors' fate. While the Prince
was alive we took greater care, salvaged more;
at times he allowed us to take home a simple
bucchero cup—but if its handle took the shape
of woman or animal, we saved it for him.

The Princess wastes no time. The *capo* curses till
we break through to the tomb of some rich old man, where
perhaps we'll find a painted vase in a hundred
pieces. All these shards are assembled, fitted
together by an artisan, fetch a high price
for the Princess.

> "After making certain that
> a certain hill—what the inhabitants
> call CUCUMELLA—was artificial,
> she chose it as the center of her
> searches. Around its base, a circle
> of no mean diameter, she began
> the excavations, . . . and the result
> far surpassed her expectations."

La Cucumella we called it, after Monte
Cacume, a huge conical peak. Much taller
before we sought out its center, the tumulus
stands amid a bare plain. In 1829
you could still see the 200-foot girdle
of stone around its base. First we dug a trench,
traced a magic circle no beast, no devil
dared cross. The ground did not resist and we turned up
more graves till some workmen caught sight of an entrance
to the mound, guarded by two sphinxes with long
tresses. Beyond them, a long passage; from its
ceiling hung bats the men singed with their lamp-flames.
Shrieks flew into the light. The sun gave no warmth.
Just above the stone belt were several small chambers,
slaves' graves we refilled with earth. We had orders
to rifle all tombs not already rifled, turned
shovel and spade to the hilltop, threw earth
to the earth. Then we struck the dead center: two
towers of massive stonework—rude, uncemented—
one round and one square. Like towers of silence.
Dumbstruck we stood, eyed by huge creatures that perched
on their crowns. I still dream of that day. Boulders
fell as from Babel, we made the sign of the cross,
ran inside for shelter, escaped with our lives.
The labyrinth led to the foot of the towers,
to the mound's heart: two modest chambers hewn out
of the living rock. From these all was gone save
the lions and gryphons above their arched doorways.
Now the whole mound is crumbling, the monsters reside
at Musignano, Bonaparte's country-seat.

The cone has been cut, leveled off to thirty feet.
The stone wall is legendary. The passageway
winds from nowhere to nowhere. The heart has caved in.

When I fell, when the vases were found, when my
oxen met their end, when the Princess gave all
the orders, when we tunneled blind like worms,
the Prince was making other observations:

> "I was just then on the point
> of completing an exploration
> of the zenithal zone above
> Senigallia . . . Using the same
> telescope with which Herschel
> discovered Uranus, we
> explored a band one half a
> celestial degree wide. We—
> I include my friend and
> collaborator of twenty years,
> Father Maurice of Brescia—
> recorded more than 20,000
> stars that exist in no prior
> catalogue. And we hope soon
> to publish our heavenly Atlas,
> which will show astronomers
> that the instrument of the great
> Sir William Herschel has not
> fallen into idle hands. . . ."

Il principe came down to earth in December
and was so taken with the antique artifacts
that he took the digging into his own hands.
Under his supervision, within four months' time
and in three to four acres surrounding
La Cucumella, 2000 *objets d'art*
were brought to light. Objects: of art? of life?
I will draw you a map of the underground
tombs without the aid of any instrument.
Subterranean constellations—The Plough,
The Oxen, The Amphora, Crown & Necklace,
Glittering Fibula, The Towers, The Sphinx—
are graven in my palms. Each winter the furrows
grow wider and deeper. When I enter the earth
I take this sky with me, an offering
to the gods of those whose graves I opened.

The Warning

*The difference between us and the Etruscans . . . is the
following: whereas we believe lightning to be released as a
result of the collision of clouds, they believe clouds collide so as
to release lightning. For as they attribute all to the deity,
they are led to believe not that things have a meaning in so
far as they occur, rather that they occur because they must
have a meaning.*

Seneca Quaestiones naturales II. 32. 2.

Open or closed my eyes
are blind. Blinded and
hollow, like shells empty
of eggs. My lips—slightly
parted—frozen, seared
shut. They want to let out
a cry: a cavernous
O. But what I saw
would not let me be
myself, troubled my
worship, made me strike
this pose.

Into my right hand
the lightning fell.
A bolt from Tinia—
it was red—I'm sure.
It glittered before
it burned and hardened
me. Was it the first
of three, the one he
hurls at will?

My sisters in worship form
a ring at my feet. But now
they beat their breasts, hands
over hearts, mourning: for me?
I raised my left hand up
toward my mouth, to stifle
its cry, cover its grimace.

The lightning slipped through
my fingers. They wrap
around Nothing now;
my thumb still points to
the sky. I was not
quick enough to see
where the clouds clashed.
Was it his second bolt—
of harm and good—cast
by consent of the Twelve
Great Gods?

Below the first ring of mourners,
a second, but here animals
join in: long necks of shrieking
gryphons, beaks open wide. They
saw it coming, too, were struck
the same as I.

The third bolt may be
thrown only by the grace
of the Nameless Ones.
It annihilates all
it touches, changes
the course of mankind.

I am not, as some say, a deity
of death. The force of the gods
shot through me, turned me into
a monument guarding charred bones.
The meaning the clay I am embodies:

O my people, I tell you
to change your lives.

Sarcophagus

Even in life my lover
said: "You sleep like a statue,
not like most people—curled up
animals."

      I can still see
the Day of Parting—perhaps
more clearly from inside this
box. At my feet, on the stone,
the journey takes form. Out there
stand two of me, one on each
side of my brother. Behind
him I touch his shoulder, bid
farewell. Before him I am
veiled, untouchable.

Dream scenes enclose me. The long recurrent
ones fret my two sides. Caught between beasts
a hart in pain: lion claws scrape his thigh,
fangs tear into his rump. The hart does
not struggle, cranes his neck, closes one eye.
A beak slashes his throat; the gryphon's
tail, a snake arched back to strike, peers into
Charun's eyes. The demon—casual,
hypnotized—leans on the hammer he has
no need to raise. His serpent hand poised,
Tuchulcha looks on, down his snout, wanting
the lion's share. . . . This much I have learned:
we creatures spoil ourselves. There is nothing
more to fear.

At my head—
dead reckoning: two Lasas
record my deeds on tablets,
on scrolls. What's done—
is done.

My right hand clasps a pomegranate whose
crimson pulp disintegrates even now;
white seeds line its comb of cells, the rind—dark
as dried blood—complete. My left hand, folded
under my cheek, has fallen asleep. I
offer myself to the stone network of
tiny mouths. . . . Above the empty space my
flesh no longer fills, my being hovers,
settles, forms a lid. As in life, I rest
there—alone—on a hard, unquiet bed.

Guardiana Della Sepoltura

On the altar, in front of the door
to Alkmene's house, the goddess sat
coiled: right leg crossed over left, fingers
interlaced. Seven days, seven
tortuous nights she locked the child
inside Alkmene's womb. Not bound
by the truth, a serving-girl said:
—Rejoice, my mistress has borne a son!
Eileithya leaped up, her arms dropped
to her sides. The charm—undone.

No hero stirs inside this house
of death shaped like a temple.
On a stone I sit outside, hands
on my knees, back straight against
the door. The roof slopes, on its ridge
two lion cubs crouch, ready.
No one can lie to the dead. With
my life I guard what goes on
within. The dead soul trapped—
be it man or woman—
can leave this house
no sooner than I walk.

Tomb of the Augurs

I *A Dog's Life*

Whose blood did I spill (if not in just
battle) to win such a fate?—a victim, my blood
a libation for the kin of a strange people.

Barefoot, blindfolded—a sack smothers
my head—I wear nothing save a scrap of lion's
skin about my loins. The Kerberos I battle,
a Molossus with a brazen voice,
fixes his teeth in my left thigh. Blood rushes down
my limbs. The master's leash winds round the massive club
in my. right hand, bridles my arms and
neck and shin. My left hand can almost reach the bone
attached to the monster's collar. . . . Can I drag him
off in time? Stave off another bite?
I strike out in the dark-

                  ness of Hades. Phersipnai—
so they call you here—you who see through the mask to
the light of the Upper World, give me
back my eyes. Let me see the tense sinews, the sleek
black coat of the beast I fight. . . . Or is the man
behind me: like Acheloös, a serpent
twining me in his coils, a charging bull—his stiff
beard jabs my arm, the masked one who urges the dog on,
is the Phersu your agent? But now
the earth trembles underfoot, for the weaker of
two wrestlers—more powerful than I—begins to
give ground.

                Mourners, weep for me, smite
                your foreheads with your palms.
                Soon I will join your charge
                behind the door.

II *Phersu*

To have been an augur! But the birds
fly away from me. . . .

                    Behind this mask
no one can see my face. My cap—tall,
visored, conical, with stiff donkey
ears—a cap of darkness. And the long,
sharp beard on my chin—is it false?

What kind of game do I master: tying
a blind man to his death, a prisoner
ignorant of our rites, a stranger
virtually unarmed? I will leave
some slack in the cord. . . .

                    But the shades
of our warriors thirst. If the cur
does not spill enough blood, I must help,
stride backward, tighten my grasp
on the leash.

            And the game goes
on, until the white cloth, patched into
the dark fabric of the jacket I wear,
takes on the color of vision: red.

Aplu

Asylum: I spread my hands
over the healing waters.
I stood on the roof ridge and
the people came. The earth still
quivers with footsteps rising,
falling, like Veii and her
kings. One hundred years I watched
counting the drops of blood shed
or let. *Lucumones*—their
faces painted vermilion,
in semicircular cloaks
the purple of the heavens
embroidered with stars—rode here,
drawn by the moon's phases. Not
golden crowns, not ivory
scepters topped with eagles in
flight could give them my vision.

> (His face is frightening, the eyes
> almonds bursting from their shells.
> The right one bulges larger, glares
> like Death. From the winged eyebrows
> down his nose the lines are sharp as
> a knife, cut through more than air.)

I have to smile. Who did they
think they were that toppled me?
Mortals! Had I not inspired
the haruspex to sing of
draining the Alban Lake, first
to himself, then to the troops,

and last before the Senate?
Those incredulous Romans—
waiting for word from Delphi!
I possess the Pythia;
what is written in the Books
of Fate she must declaim:
                    O
Roman   let not the Alban water remain in its lake
Let it not flow to the sea in its natural channel
Disperse it in rivulets   Draw it through your fields
You shall stand victor on the walls of Veii.

                    (His lips are swollen, the lower
                    cleft like his chin. The corners
                    of the mouth point down so that
                    the smile is almost a grimace.
                    Long black plaits snake down his back,
                    fall forward on his shoulders.
                    But the delicate, conical
                    ears are exposed, open to all.)

Marcus Furius Camillus,
I heard your command to
dig the *cuniculus,* to
undermine the *arx.* The hand
of a soldier burned like my
own, snatched the hot entrails off
the altar. Your army swarmed
through the citadel, wrenched bolts
from the city gates, flooded
over the walls. From rooftops
untouched by the breathing flames
women hurled tiles down on them,
tore their hair for the children's
cries rose like smoke, shrieks blacker
than slaughter. It was not long
before the shrine beneath me
caught fire and collapsed. I lay
in the soil. Better to lie
underground two thousand years . . .
Vulca, who made me, shaped your
faceless gods. Where are they now
Camillus? Even your ruins
have perished.

(His hands are lost, but the biceps
burn with strength. The pectorals high
and developed. On the muscular
legs the veins stand out. Supported
by the lyre, he is walking toward me.)

I did not die, I darkened
like a riverbed currents
cut and waters heal. I'll sing
my hands out of the earth and
call them to me. I do not
long for the soil, but for
the touch, the call of the hand
that made me.

(Here, in the Villa Giulia,
I weep. And the waters heal.)

Canopic Jar

From Sebek's dark waters,
erect in a lotus flower,
the sons of Horus stand
before Osiris' throne.

Human-headed, I am like Imseti,
who held the liver—the seat
of life. Those remains most vital
to the living rot the dead.

I am harder and I hold all of a dead
man in my round body. So light
his ashes would not weigh an ostrich
feather. But they *are* the truth:

The dead cannot be judged.
Thin as the border of life
and death, my lips seal the dead,
keep their secret from you.

Woman from Chianciano

My child won't stir,
stares up at me all
supplication. Arms
close to his sides, knees
bent, his tiny feet rest
on an arm of this
chair. Swaddled in cloth
not thick enough to
warm, perhaps he sleeps.
I neither sleep nor
move: I hold him on
my thighs, the weight of
his head on my strong
right arm, his body
in my two huge hands
that press firmly and
softly into his
formless back. My eyes
are open, fix on empty
space. They cannot see
his smile of trust. Still,
we are one, this knowledge
surges through the stone.

The arms of my throne,
twin watchdogs, sphinxes'
wings; thick hair
bound and crowned, their heads
press against my knees.
They gape—one in surprise,
the other in dismay.

They hold me here
unmoving as the folds
of cloth that fall
resolutely, cushion,
and hem me in.
                    Inside
I can feel some other
shape, older than my own:
A woman's head that once
served wine, now holds dust
and bones of a child
not yet born.

Vortex

Circling me, as ants their sacred hill,
an infestation, an army of bronze.
Tiny men—hunters, warriors with spears
and shields—naked, take part in ritual
dance. And I, the beast, collared, captive,
chained, made to sit on my rump—
I stretch my paws, my claws out toward them.
They will be my catch.

I am life, center of the universe,
dangerous to idolaters of the dead.
Life, animal, animal, spirit, god,
I have no need of weapons or of tools.
What I crave I take barehanded. I am
the omphalos toward which all members rise.

Do they aim to numb me, to stun me with
mere dance? I can still count them as they pass.
The inner circle held eight, holds seven
now and a pair of feet. Arms reach out
to embrace, end in fists clenched tight.
The outer ring has nine with room to spare;
a few have left the ranks. Still, the trusty
ploughman guides his long-horned ox. I would not
touch, not harm the beast.

Absurd to sit here chained. They mean
to kill me, to draw their life from mine.
My eyes bulge huge and placid and intent.
My mouth grows wider, deeper, wears a grin.
The circle narrows and I take them in.

Porta all'Arco, Volterra

It is a deep old gateway, almost a tunnel, with the outer arch
facing the desolate country . . . . and three dark heads, now
worn featureless, reach out cunningly and inquiringly, one
from the keystone of the arch, one from each of the arch
bases, to gaze from the city and into the steep hollow of the
world beyond.

D. H. *Lawrence*, Etruscan Places

Your climb was long. Pause here and rest by this
our gateway. Three ancient heads of dark gray
peperino speak as the single genius
of the place. Though our lineaments blur, wear
down into the stone—appear as they were
before we taught the carver to cut lines—
our lips receding into formlessness,
still we'll tell you of the city's founding.
We, the patron deities, inform all
things of Velathri, and still watch on. Our
eyes, patient eyes of stone, for ever set
on the signs and portents, the earth and sky.

Lightning forks the dark, points to the ground but does
not strike, flashes, and flashing turns in a ring
of fire that caps the peak of one pale, spiny
hill. Tinia still has his throne above its crown,
his eyes bright beacons focussed on the South.
His left hand draws the stars across the sky.
His right hand wields the deep red thunderbolt.
Then, as now, he let the levin fall, gave us
a sign. By the flickering light we read
the shifting lines of his palm: a map of

Velathri, the city that would spread in
concentric rings around the spiny hill.

Knowing this, we called out to the people
who dwelt scattered in the mountain gorges,
spoke in the voice of thunder the god's command:
You men who live here, gather your families,
your livestock, your household gods. Shovels in
hand, scale that spiny hill; on its top, lay
down the *groma*, fix the cardinal points;
then descend to the circle of its base.
There you must dig a trench into which your
kinfolk shall cast the first fruits of all things,
and also a handful of soil from each
of your native lands. Mingle the fruits and earth
in the trench, the *mundus;* mind you seal it well
with the hill's own stones. This be the sacred
shaft, the innermost circle of Velathri.

The *mundus* sealed, we called on a ploughman:
Founder, go fetch a white bull and cow, each one
strong and unblemished. Yoke them together; shoe
your plough with a brazen share, for you shall cut
the line of Velathri's wall. Our voice will
guide you. Facing North, stand behind the beasts,
the cow to your left hand, the bull to your right.
Just as the sun, from East to West, describes
a broad arc in the heavens, so you shall trace
that arc upon the earth. The share will cut
a deep, clean furrow. Those who follow your trail
will turn the clods inward, toward the city's heart.
This line is sacred; do not cross it now
or ever. Those who try—know them to be
your foes—they will be struck by lightning, like
Capaneus scaling the wall of Thebes. Now
for the gates (ours but one of three) you must
lift up the plough, break the sacred line and leave
vacant space. Else you shall die imprisoned
in your city.

Pause now and rest, look down with us and see
the map of valley, river, plain, the lay
of the land below. Look down from this verge
and see where your dead shall lie. Beyond the line

of the wall shall circle ring upon ring
of graves. You will be safe inside the wall's
circuit, gathered around the *mundus*, gate
to the underworld.

Tomorrow you shall cut the boundary stones,
all the local stones: soft, sandy, yellow
panchina; dense-grained, dark peperino,
hard, semi-crystalline travertino.
You may measure their length by the span of your
outstretched arms, their height by the breadth of your chest.
But you must gather them up in your arms,
embrace them. It is the human touch that
sanctifies the stones.

Traveler, remember us by the coin
of the realm: a three-inch round, cast copper,
on the reverse a dolphin engulfed by
the name: ΙϹΟΑϞ϶϶ on the obverse, capped
by a petasos, a beardless Janus-head.

From Vetulonia

These cannot speak for themselves
so I'll speak for them,
bound to each other with a triple chain:

> found loose in the earth
> above a circular tomb,
> a man and his woman, roughly
> four inches high. He,
> a head taller, stands a short
> distance from her, needn't
> lift a finger to keep her
> within range.

> Their elliptical heads angle
> back, jaws project; ears,
> round and flat, cling to the long,
> thick necks. In profile like axeheads
> rising out of two bundles of rods: even
> more like apes' skulls—beasts
> from the neck up;

> down below

> her broad shoulders, high
> on her narrow chest, small,
> rounded, prominent breasts. Her arms
> corset her ribcage. His, caught
> in the chain, are suppressed.

The bronze links run
from the end of her braid
to his elbows, almost graze
the tip of his large, erect
phallus. She leans forward;
her knees are locked. He holds
himself upright by tilting back.

Seen from one side, the coupling
is terribly clear: with no chain
between them, they'd be inseparable.

Pars Sinistra (Familiaris)

*If you must rest in a grave,
let it be the Etruscan one.*

Freud

The Mummy Speaks

Mummy of a young woman (with wrappings removed)
standing in a glass case and held upright by an iron rod.
Another glass case contains the mummy's bandages which
are completely covered with writing in an unknown and
hitherto undeciphered language . . .

What did you take me for, Michael
Baric, that day in Alexandria
in eighteen hundred forty-eight?
Did you expect to be taken? Palmed off
with a bundle of sticks, rubbish,
sawdust, cats' skeletons, stuffed by human
hand into a non-human skin
in the back street of a Cairo bazaar?
Even my case is real. You set
it on end in your salon, telling
the credulous ladies it held
the sister of King Stephen
of Hungary! You never looked
inside. Later, you died, left me
to your brother, Elias, pastor
in some godforsaken Slavonian
village. He reviled me, packed me off
to Agram, where they dishoused, stripped
and catalogued me: "an outstanding
treasure of the National Museum."

The iron rod eats into what little
flesh I have left. And I'm cold.
Cold comfort my words, unstrung
in a case nearby.

ceia hia . . .
ceia hia etnam ciz vacl trin velthre

And the linguists who came to visit
not me, but my wrappings: Herr Doktor
Heinrich Brugsch, and that beastly
Sir Richard Burton! *Narren,* fools,
I say, thinking my words, my letters,
"partly Greco-European and
partly Runic," or Arabic
translation from the Book of the Dead.

male ceia hia etnam ciz vacl aisvale
male ceia hia trinth etnam ciz ale

More than one man of the cloth has laid
hands on me. The museum director,
the abbé Ljubic, removed my bandages
to his study, but not before he'd
dispensed great lengths of them to his
congregation. Scattering the gods
whose wills they could not read. And here
I shrivel, my toes curl, my chin—
sharp as a knife—cuts my sternum.

male ceia hia etnam ciz vacl vile vale

What nonsense I have heard these many
years through the transparent walls
of this rigid case! Even a man of
instinct, Jacob Krall, could not take
my words at face value, took them
first to Vienna, suspecting the ink,
the linen of forgery. When he was
sure—my words are Etruscan—
I was cross-examined:
—Is she Egyptian?
—Why bury a book with a girl?
—Is she Etruscan?
—Why wind the strips so that the writing touches her flesh?

staile itrile bia ciz trinthaśa śacnitn

They photographed my words under
infrared light, made transcriptions,
exposed them to questioning eyes.
Trying to trace my words through tangled
roots, who sought to render them
fell into deepest night. One heard cries
rising from the cloth. Another saw
sacrifice to a vulture god. I danced
before them: a witch, a troll, or served
my ancestors an insubstantial meal.

Have they considered that without me
the text has no meaning? Our language
was reserved: we spoke only among
ourselves. Is this why they parted us:
afraid I would take every sign
away from them? The bitumen that
seeped through my skin and into the cloth
transformed the words. They entered my flesh,
became whole inside me. Black ink on
white cloth: opaque remains. The meanings
lie in the lacunae.

God's Breath

Inside and outside black, straight
through the clay. Fired slowly,
in low, even, smoking heat.
Children of ovens. Receptacles
on feet. Our provenance? We will
speak true. Among Etruscan ware
we are the Jews: Survivors
bound by god-given laws. And like
Shem's sons, misunderstood because
form free of context, bygone
ritual, is seen as evil
or made trivial.

Footwarmers. Fumigators. Tea
sets with cups, bowls, spoons, stray
calling cards. Ladies' toilettes!
Take no one's words but ours.
Bucchero nero e pesante—
clay breathed black and deep—
exhaled, sung by a god. Burnished
to a hard metallic sheen,
we lit the caverns, without
fuel we burned. Strange braziers:
Hearth, Stove, Focus, Home.
Warm on our rims and

handles, dark of our dark,
beasts, birds, women's heads
shine silver-black, break
into song.

La Defunta

Tomba del Barone, Tarquinia

The chamber is not wide. The double pitch
ceiling slopes from either side of the roofbeam
which is painted red. In the pediments:
false corbels shaped like altars. Not to be
slaughtered on them, dolphins, panthers, motley
hippocampi overlook a figured frieze.

Who cannot walk through this room, frozen
stiff as an Egyptian obelisk,
her arms raised in greeting (in warning):
She fills the room with her presence and
absence.
Kybele? Ceres? Persephone?
A shadow veiled and crowned, her contours
melt into the stone wall's ground, as if
in cloud. His arm round a young boy's neck,
a man in a short black chiton walks
toward her, ministering. To the boy she speaks:

—I have come to hear you play. How sweet
your song, even the saplings tremble
to hear. No wonder he holds you close,
closer than the wine he offers me.

Your air holds me still as soil the roots
of trees. But the music from your double
pipes moves me, and we meet on the same black
ground (red underlies it; for you all
things are red: the steeds, the foliage,
my veil—reflections of your red world),
the same black ground in which my trees take

root and rise. Their leaves are blue, silvered
like those on the olive trees outside
in the strong sun and wind. Cool, brilliant,
opaque. And this stalk of bulbs that rise
one from the other, of their own accord,
reaching just a bit higher than the notes
you sound, it divides your ground from mine.
Put the flute down, my child, I can teach . . .

Wait, look around you at what your life may
be. Horsemen—their hair white as their horses'
manes, as your hair, my boy—red-skinned, sparsely
clad in dark red pallia, mounted
rivals who hold whips with barbed handles
in their closed hands, race for the bright red
garlands hanging there, just beyond their
reach.
   Give me your hand.
        Look there—

They have dismounted and are arguing.
Each leads his horse by the bridle, from
each man's arm a garland hangs.
         Turn

and see behind you, on the other wall,
how they go on. Shouting, they raise their arms,
as if to summon me. But my image
fades between them. The outcome is not my
concern. I have not come to judge the game,
but to offer life of a different kind.

Your music calls and brings me here.
My steeds are black as your father's beard.
My steeds obey song, their hoofs are blue.
Come, I shall drink from the kylix, you
from my open hand.

Hand to Hand

Ivory, brittle, older
than all the others,
nails bitten, digits
split by water, air, decay.
Our forearms—they held the tang
of a mirror, a fan—crawl with life:
Vines tangle. A centaur with human
legs has a lion by the tail.
Gryphons' beaks gape. Sphinxes
keep their secrets.

Attached to bone-thin
arms we raked the coals.
We may be small, but
nothing slips through
our fingers, supple
as asps side by side.
Front and back show
palms. To you a signal.
To the face of fire
a caress.

Can you still see the rings,
ten narrow bands girdling
our fingers? Tarnished.
The stones have fallen away.
Our broad backs toward you
say we have something to hide.
Inside we are hollow; our
palms are blank. Ten overlong,

delicate fingers rise up
like cypress.

Two rows of golden studs
hammered into our knuckles.
Thumbs broken off. These palms
were leather once. Gold nails
join our wrists to bronze cuffs.

> Larger than need be,
> first to know pain,
> too often empty of
> a palm frond, shield
> or spear, a single flower,
> a brazen patera,
> an axe, a thunderbolt,
> a bird with horns,
> an egg, a pomegranate,
> the beloved's shoulders,
> the double pipes,
> the power to give . . .

Gone from these hands
that life has left.

The Stonecutter

Is not this rock-face one huge shapeless mass
that cries for our hands to mold it? To shape
a temple for the gods, yet for ourselves,
within the body's limits. Transient,
mutable, soft. Soft stone, most human stone,
hard as sinews, hard enough to sustain
grandeur on the Greek model, but not cold,
white, polished smooth. Warm stone against my palms,
tufa that glows red in sunset, red as
the setting sun, your pores drink water, breathe
the open air. Down there, where the river
flows and the sheep graze, I'll cut channels to
carry the excess off, that it may fall
into the waiting palm of the Hand of Earth.
High and steep these hillsides the river has
cut into cliffs. The long stone face bids me
construct a staircase a god could climb—
a god whose stride surpasses the human.
Three steps will place his footsoles in the sky.
From the highest plain (the uppermost stair)
a priest will pour libations, sanctify
the ground. Whoever crosses this bridge will
have a sure footing, leave no tracks behind.
To enter the temple would be our death:
the porous stone so full of the being
of him who can scale the three huge stairs from
outside. On their facades I'll carve false doors.
Only the gods themselves can open them.
Doors that lead to what we do not know, can
never know; hard as we try to see behind
the wall that keeps us always to one side.

at Norchia

To one side
of the temple
   I'll hew a
narrow stairway
      a man can
descend. Narrow
      and long this
path to the foot
         of the cliff.
There I'll hollow
   a cave: charmed
   hushed, magical.
         Its man-made
   mouth will be sealed
         with a stele
      on which the priest
            shall inscribe
      the words no man
            may utter.
      Words that protect
            the dead from
            unclean spirits.
               There I shall
      lay my dead. None
               but the Hand
      of Earth may touch
                  them, gather
               them in its grasp.

Nothing our own hands fashion
endures intact. Weather will
have its way, eating into
these faces, making queer shapes
of our work. And some future
race will worry these contours,
forcing open its false doors.
None but the Hand of Sky—palm
blazoned with thunderbolts, streaked
with burning stars—on the day
it clasps the Hand of Earth
(crushing our bones to powder)
can bring the temple down.

Fabric of Ceremony

One who plays the pipes.
A priest with a pointed hat.
                         (*Turn!*)
A young man waving a branch
toward two who stretch a veil

                         over
those whose fates be joined.

        Facing us, their faces concealed,
        masked by the ample drape; below
        their hips they've nothing
        (a fragment—the tablet broken):
        three unquestionably bound.

And those who pull the leaf, the canopy
of life, so like a long, fringed cloth—
why does the one caress it,
his smile almost religious?
Does his other arm prop up
the man whose face is blank?

        Is it the man? Near shapeless,
        this couple, each of whom plants
        one hand on the crucial figure:
        A matchmaker? The bride's father?
        A tree trunk deeply incised.
        They clutch it to steel themselves.
        As if to learn how, blind, two
        may strike root as one, through
        stony, hard-packed soil.

Hut Urn

So deep in the earth,
below layers of ash, of tufa,
you might never find me,
but for the tumulus:

That huge mound of earth
—girded by stones,
on a stone base—
mimics my roof.

Open my door. In the gable
peer through the smokehole. Inside
I am dark as the artificial cave
you entered searching for me.

The house *is* the body I tell you.
I am the house of fired clay.
I hold the ashes of the woman
who lived in a hut of daubed clay.

The tombs plough their way underground,
below that perishable earthen roof.
The stone mouth narrows,
recedes, disintegrates.
                           Out of reach
I hold myself whole.

Gorgoneion

*But the wonder of ancient wonders in the Museum of
Cortona, is a bronze lamp of such surpassing beauty and
elaboration of workmanship as to throw into the shade every
toreutic work yet discovered in the soil of Etruria . . . It is
circular, about twenty-three inches in diameter, hollow like
a bowl . . . Round the rim are sixteen lamps, of classic
form, fed by oil from the great bowl . . . The bottom is hol-
lowed in the center, and contains a huge Gorgon's face . . .
Here is no loveliness—all horror.*

George Dennis, The Cities and Cemeteries of Etruria

Not since my sister's slaughter, since the birth
of Pegasos and Chrysaor, have I
spoken a word. Awakened by stifled cries,
Euryale and I went bounding after—
what? Winged sandals thrashing the pathless air,
the glint of a helmet that we could not touch,
a leather pouch out of which all pain issued . . .

So many years ago my own voice failed, so many
years my tongue's lolled from my mouth, my eyes
stared from their sockets, turning to stone
only those by nature deaf and blind. Now I'll
cut tusk from tooth and speak my mind:

> The pain that keeps me separate makes
> me hard. They do not think, who crouch
> around my rim, piping their scorching airs,
> of anything. On the utmost circuit, far—
> far from all care, they turn from me

in horror, not to stone but into
the animals they are:

Satyrs, squat goaty men who play
the syrinx or the tibia, hard
in their lips, their beards, their
lower parts. Sirens who pinch
their breasts and spread their wings
in proud allure; their sooty mouths
agape in silent choir. Peering
out above each wing and shoulder,
Acheloös, bearded bull-man,
horned voyeur.

Under the satyrs' feet, fat dolphins run,
sporting on seawaves, frigid hooklike curls.
Under the water's circle: earth's perfect
sphere. Creatures feeding on creatures,
tooth and nail, sinking their fangs
or struggling: lion, leopard, boar, wolf,
stag, horse, gryphon; the common round.

And I, the Gorgon, central, grim, and sound —
immortal, not a god. These eyes have seen
a plethora of fear, are terror complacent,
pain endured. My mind is clear: clear
oil, life's vital blood. A wreath of asps,
tight crimping strands of hair set my scalp,
my brain, my heart on fire. And when I think,
memory lights these wicks, makes passion
run and burn from sphere to sphere: fire
of earth, of water, and of air. I, Sthenno,
mete out equal shares to all quick creatures,
though they be unaware — knowing no pain,
no joy, no heat, no chill — creatures of habit,
having no force or will. I give their life
its fire, and hold still.

Calchas, Haruspex

To work now. The day grows
warm. Off with these vestments—
mere tokens of office—the fringed
mantle closed with a fibula,
the narrow tunic, the high cap
with a wide base and cylindrical
crown. Is it not best to read
Their wills in Their image—
even the Veiled, the Nameless Ones?
These heavy sandals! That's better,
the earth is cool underfoot.

Long before sunrise I
sanctified the grove. Here lie
the sacred stone, the victim
slaughtered. I pull out
the liver; cupped in my left palm
it begins to cool. Early morning:
the slant rays of the sun
expose the gland's sixteen zones.

My left foot rests on the boulder
(from whose sector of the sky,
I wonder, did *it* fall?), left
elbow on left thigh; perpendicular
to the stone, my right foot planted
squarely on the ground.

The lobes of the gland point
down, hang like pouches,

hang like a woman's breasts.
The fingers of my right hand
stroke the moist surface, probe
cysts, search out deformations.

> *Tages, aid me in my task.*
> *The organ feels soft. Boiled,*
> *It might dissolve. I cannot*
> *Yet tell how this day will end.*

II

The sky, the templum, seems
overcast. High clouds streak
the Northwest. Not clouds
overhead—wings—enormous
wings shoot out of my shoulders!

Have I become a demon
who guides the dead to
Death's door? A harbinger,
whose fate will I foretell?
An agent of fate,
will I drive the nails
that end our years
into the wall
of the Temple of Nortia?

But the Fates, the Lasas,
are female. Winged beauties,
I have seen them cross the sky,
scrolls in their hands,
blind to everything
but their destination.

A priest, I know the Discipline:
how to defer the End of Days
(ten years for a man,
thirty for our people)
through prayer, sacrifice,
propitiation.

No time for those now. These wings
the pronouncement, myself
the prodigy—the last sign
I will read.

>   *When the liver falls*
>   *from my left hand, this one*
>   *of the ten saecula granted*
>   *us, the Rasenna, will end.*

Final Questions

Is the route safe? Why
this armed guide, a wingless
guardian with thick thighs,
a bow, two naked arrows? Why
this haste? Won't our goal
last?

Putting your soul
into another's hands—
no easy matter.
Of spirit alone,
he may not know, may
not care to hold you
without hurting you
out of harm's way. How
to carry you (where?).
He runs too swiftly.
The wings at his ankles
blur.

I watch my body walk
away from me.
Swarthy companions—
one bears a spear—
surround, enfold,
encompass her.

Maybe I am safe, am saved
and the path is clear.
It is not a man in whose

arms I am snared but
Artemis, appeased.
The air we travel
cradles us.

O Mother, take me
to safety.
To certainty.

La Banditaccia, 1979

A bright, hot day. Late June. The bus from Rome
passed a seaside town—Ladispoli—plagued
by commerce, blessed with a breeze from the sea.
But from Cerveteri the Tyrrhenian
has receded far. Caere it was called
when the Gauls sacked Rome. The Vestal Virgins
took refuge on its high plateau, rising
in steep cliffs above the plain of the coast.
The small, modern village has given up
its ghosts. Peasants follow their ploughs, shepherds
their flocks, unaware of the city trod,
buried underfoot.

From the parched, walled town a road winds ALLE
NECROPOLI. I have come here to walk
the streets of that parallel city, home
of Caere's dead. Dense vegetation masks
the roadside tombs. I find and enter one.
Insects, the color of grass, swarm the dark
entrance. Inside: gray water, ankle-deep;
shallow benches. A sideshow, not the site
I know from Lawrence, Dennis, photographs
and maps. The road seems too long in the heat.
Lost in its ditch, the trickling Manganello
is nowhere in sight.

At the Zone, as in recurrent dreams of
houses, corridors, doors to be opened,
I cross the threshold of a concrete hut,
decipher a sign that says *la grotta*

bella, The Tomb of the Reliefs, is sealed,
closed for repairs. (In my sleep I'd know its
single square chamber with a gabled lid,
its pillowed niches for the important dead,
their household objects stuccoed on the walls.)
A rite of passage, this disappointment;
undeterred, I set foot on the ancient
burial ground.

Just there, outside the first huge cinctured mound,
the tiny markers of women, of men:
stone houses, stone cippi. Like women and
men, opaque, unenterable. The mounds
can be entered. Their doorways, dark mouths, call
me inside. Unasked-for, a guide: "Look at
these marks on the stone couch that runs around
the room. These, shaped like keyholes; men's corpses
covered them." Not keyholes, but phalluses
incised in the stone. "Women lay on plain
benches, safe in sarcophagi or clothes."
Afraid to take my arm, he points out holes
in the floor and the darker alcoves where
the rich rotted in their jewels. I follow
because I need his eyes, his legs that know
when a passageway leads to light.

Into blinding light we come. Seared by sun,
all along the sunken path, jewels are strewn.
Huge stones, bright, hot, cheap, lichen-crusted: red,
gray, amber, green. And the path leads between
mountainous tumuli, shrub-covered, girt
with stones, leveled or high, overgrown with
blooms, grassy, or wearing cypress trees as
feathers in their caps. As once, perhaps, they
wore towers crowned by the creatures that lived
in their makers' dreams.

Here a long range of sepulchres, a block
of flats, stands square in the sun. Out of one,
come to life from a painted wall, a black
bird swiftly flies. Inside these simple tombs,
all not shield or seat or bier carved into
the living rock, all not secured is gone.

Inside: bright yellow stagnant water; wild
green algae swirl through it in those contours
Etruscans traced remembering the waves
of the sea. A flood of memory. Tides
turn, go out.

A different race left only
a name: La Banditaccia. Unattached.
Abandoned. *Terra bandita,* land set
apart; because the ground is broken though
unfarmed, that ending of ugliness, "accia,"
was tacked on. Into its fissures lives withdrew.
As rain, as flood, the sea seals its wounds.
The place is whole, all of one piece. Broken
ground, uninhabited, pure space.

Degli Sposi

Of us
not much is known.
Our lives were not
extraordinary.
Our silence seals
a deeper silence.

Sharing the single bed, how close
we lie; fingers curved over palms
whose fable reads: *conjugal bliss
is possible.*

How simple it was. It is.
But the secret's lost. That's why
you look to us, how we carry
ourselves, our smile. We live
in that space where all's yet
to become: embrace—a tenderness,
an expectation, myth, tentative
gesture preceding touch. Before
the shock of contact, when caution
counsels: Leave.

Not at all easy, this, to speak
of love. And to survive. Our skin
glows red with passion in reserve.
Unbridled, it would deaden every
nerve. Feeling—the reins, the check,
restraint, repose, out of whose thousand
fragments we are restored. Loving

each other even after death. As if
life were not, had not been, enough.

We touch, we hold, we keep
one another free.

Notes

The Twelve

In reference to the peoples who, for some seven centuries, held what is essentially modern Tuscany, the ancient authors speak of *duodecim populi Etruriae*—the twelve peoples or cities of Etruria, or of *omnis Etruria*—all Etruria. Once a year the heads of the twelve autonomous city-states are said to have met at the *Fanum Voltumnae*, the sanctuary of the god Voltumna, which has not yet been found. Judging from the wars they sometimes waged on one another, the "League" of Twelve was a loose one. The annual meeting of the *duodecim populi*, who shared a common language (still undeciphered), was probably more a religious gathering than a political one. Furthermore, the membership of the "League" seems to have varied; in imperial times mention is made of as many as fifteen peoples. A list, by no means exclusive, of the cities which probably belonged to the "League" at one time or another would have to include: Arretium (modern Arezzo), Caere (Cerveteri), Clusium (Chiusi), Cortona, Faesulae (Fiesole), Perusia (Perugia), Populonia (Porto Baratti), Rusellae (Roselle), Tarquinii (Tarquinia), Veii (Veio), Vetulonia, Volaterrae (Volterra), Volsinii (Bolsena), and Vulci. There were several other centers of Etruscan activity and much evidence of Etruscan expansion as far north as Bologna, as far south as Campania.

The Discipline

All of the Etruscan books to which the ancient Romans refer have been lost to us, and so we must rely on late and biased testimony pertaining to the revealed religion of the Etruscans and their practice of it. The *disciplina etrusca*, the body of laws and rituals by which the Etruscans maintained good relations with their gods, is said to have been revealed to them mainly by Tages (the son of Genius and grandson of Jupiter), and partly by a nymph called Vegoia or Begoe. Ancient authors speak of the *Libri Tagetici* (Books of Tages), or more specifically of the *Libri Fulgurales* (dealing with the interpretation of lightning), the *Libri Haruspicini* (concerning the scrutiny of livers of sacrificial victims), the *Libri Fatales* (dealing with Fate), the *Libri Rituales* (for founding cities and temples, surveying fields, sanctifying space), as well as other lost books. I shall refer to these books in subsequent notes to the poems.

Pars Dextra (Hostilis)

The poems in this book have been arranged in accordance with the Etruscan conception of the *templum caeleste*. See the note to "Porta all' Arco, Volterra," and the diagrammatic contents on page 87.

I "A Handle on Things" (p. 17)

Charun: Not the pleasant ferryman of the Greeks (Charon), but an underworld demon generally portrayed as a hideous old man with flaming eyes, a hooked nose, the ears and often the tusks of a beast. Frequently he is represented with wings, but his chief attribute is a hammer or mallet with which he perhaps crushed the skull of the dying or the dead.

Tages, the Law, Tarchon: In the neighborhood of Tarquinia, a peasant was ploughing the land and cut an unusually deep furrow, from which sprang Tages, who had the appearance of a boy and the gray hair of a sage. According to one tradition, the ploughman himself was Tarchon, the legendary founder of Tarquinia. According to another, Tarchon was but one of the twelve *lucumones* or *principis* (priest-kings, or heads) of "all Etruria," who came running at the ploughman's cry of astonishment. Chanting, Tages revealed the *disciplina etrusca* [see headnote], and those who were present wrote it down.

II "Lucien's Ploughman 1848" (p. 18)

"That small bronze model": The "ploughman of Arezzo" (*aratore di Arezzo*) in the Museo di Villa Giulia [henceforward Villa Giulia], Rome, dates from c. 400 BC. See also note to "A Handle on Things," Tages.

Lucien Bonaparte (1775–1840), Napoleon's brother, was made Prince of Canino by Pius VII. The lands cost him 40,000 louis. His lines come from his catalogue raisonné: *Museum Etrusque*, fouilles de 1828 à 1829, Vases Peints Avec Inscriptions; Viterbe, chez Camille Tosoni imprimeur, 1829.

Nenfro: a compact, dark gray, hard variety of tufa (a volcanic stone).

Bucchero: unglazed, unpainted black (or gray) pottery typical of Etruscan archaism and subarchaism, generally imitating the forms of metal receptacles; when thin-walled it is called *bucchero sottile,* when thick-walled it is *bucchero pesante.*

III "The Warning" (p.23)

The speaking object is a terracotta ossuary from Chiusi, dating from c. 600 BC; in the Museo Nazionale Etrusco (formerly Museo Civico), Chiusi.

"A bolt from Tinia": Tinia was the supreme deity of the Etruscans (analogous to the Greek Zeus). The *Libri Fulgurales,* a part of the Etruscan Discipline, dealt with the rules for the observation and interpretation of thunderbolts. He who read the wills of the gods as manifested in lightning was called a *fulguriator,* or, in Etruscan, *trutnvt frontac.* Each of the *Novensiles,* the Nine Great Gods who could hurl thunderbolts, had his or her own distinctive bolt. Tinia alone could hurl three sorts of red lightning. The first, which he could throw at his own discretion, was called *fulmen praesagum.* The second, the *fulmen ostentorium,* could be thrown only with the consent of the Twelve Great Gods—*Dii Consentes* or *Complices*—six of either sex, who formed the council of Tinia. In order to cast the third bolt, the *fulmen peremptorium,* the effects of which were always harmful, Tinia required the consent of the *Dii Superiores et Involuti*—superior and shrouded in mystery. These were the terrible gods whose names were hidden; they ruled over gods and men, and even Tinia had to obey their decrees.

IV "Sarcophagus" (p.25)

> . . . *Und sieh die halbe Sicherheit des Vogels*
> *der beinah beides weiß aus seinem Ursprung,*
> *als wär er eine Seele der Etrusker,*

aus einem Toten, den ein Raum empfing,
doch mit der ruhenden Figur als Deckel. . . .

Rainer Maria Rilke, *Duineser Elegien*, VIII.

The speaking object is the lid of a *nenfro* sarcophagus
from Tarquinia, dating from the fourth century BC; in the
Ny Carlsberg Glyptotek, Copenhagen.

    Tuchulcha: Another fearsome underworld
demon often represented with the face of a bird of prey,
the ears of a donkey, and with menacing snakes in his
hair or hands.

    Lasa (also *lasa*, pl. *lasae*): A goddess of Fate,
generally represented with wings, sometimes with a ham-
mer and nail, but more frequently with a bottle in one
hand and a stylus in the other.

V *"Guardiana Della Sepoltura"* (p. 27)

The speaking object is a limestone cinerary urn in the
shape of a house guarded by what may be a Lasa, from
Chiusi, c. 400 BC, 55 cm high; in the British Museum,
London.

    Alkmene was the mother of Herakles. Hera
sent Eileithya (or the Eileithyai), the goddess of child-
birth, to postpone the hero's birth. Ovid tells not only of
the sending of Lucina (Eileithya) to work the delay, but
also of the goddess' transformation of Alkmene's servant,
Galanthis, into a weasel.

VI *"Tomb of the Augurs"* (p. 28)

The richly painted "Tomb of the Augurs," which dates
from the last quarter of the sixth century BC, was discov-
ered in April 1878 at Tarquinia by Luigi Dasti. Appar-
ently he mistook the bird-surrounded mourners on the
tomb's rear wall (who stand to either side of a painted
door, representing the entrance to the abode of the dead)
for augurs. The speakers of this poem reside on the right
wall of the tomb, where are portrayed funereal games in
honor of the dead.

    Kerberos: The hound of hell; according to
Hesiod he had "a voice of bronze and fifty heads." In
most depictions of Herakles harrowing Hell and bringing
back Kerberos, the hound has only three heads.

    Molossus: A Molossian dog or hound, a
kind of mastiff.

Phersipnai: Etruscan form of Persephone.

Acheloös: A river god who could change his shape, and whom Herakles had to master in wrestling in order to win Deïaneira. In doing so Herakles broke off one of Acheloös's horns. In Etruscan art Acheloös is sometimes represented as a bull; but more often his head, bearded and horned, is seen in the center of bronze shields (hailing from Tarquinia and dating from the end of the sixth century BC).

Phersu: The Etruscan name corresponds to the Latin word *persona*, meaning "a masked figure." The "phersu" is also seen on the left wall of this tomb and on the walls of two other tombs at Tarquinia.

VII "Aplu" (p. 30)

Aplu: The Etruscan appellation of Apollo. The Apollo of Veii (c. 515–490 BC) is a larger than life-size terracotta statue which stands in Room VII of the Villa Giulia in Rome. It was found at the Portonaccio sanctuary or precinct (outside and to the west of the ancient city walls), by chance, on 19 May 1916, when C. Q. Giglioli was directing exploratory excavations while on a brief leave from military service at the front.

"the healing waters": The sanctuary at Portonaccio was clearly connected with the cult of health-giving waters. To one side of the excavated temple is a large pool lined with closely fitted tufa blocks; to this day the pool is almost perfectly preserved.

"Veii and her kings": For nearly four centuries Veii was Rome's rival in military power, fighting no fewer than fourteen wars with her.

Lucumones (pl., sg. *lucumo*): The priest-kings of Etruria. Four times a year the *lucumo* of each city would show himself in public, riding forth in a chariot drawn by white horses, and then performing sacrifices. In the Fifth War between Veii and Rome, the Veientes joined the rest of the Etruscan "League," but were defeated by Tarquinius Priscus (a Roman king of Etruscan extraction) and were forced to sue for peace. In token of submission the cities of the "League" had to send him the Etruscan insignia of authority, which included the purple robe, the *corona aurea*, the scepter surmounted by an eagle, the *sella curulis* (an ivory folding seat), and the twelve *fasces* of the lictors. Following the expulsion of the Tarquins, the Roman Republican magistrates took up these symbols.

Haruspex: See note to "Calchas, Haruspex."

Camillus: The Roman general, who, after a ten-year siege, captured Veii by artifice in 396 BC. For the story of the *cuniculus*, or mine, of Camillus, see *Liv.* V. 19ff.

Arx: The highest part of the city and/or its citadel. Aplu's temple was not the *arx* but was located outside the city walls.

Vulca: The only name of an Etruscan artist that has come down to us. He was summoned to Rome to fashion the cult image for the temple of the Capitoline Jupiter (dedicated 509 BC) and also made the middle acroterium of the temple, which represented Jupiter standing on a quadriga.

VIII "Canopic Jar" (p. 33)

The speaking object is from Cetona (near Chiusi), of clay, dated 550–500 BC, stands 61 cm high, and is in the Museo Archeologico, Florence. "Canopic" jars, vases, or urns—the name has been taken from Egyptian zoomorphic or anthropomorphic jars called Canopic—did not, in Etruria, hold the viscera of the mummified dead; rather, they held the ashes of the cremated.

Sebek: The Egyptian crocodile god. The four Sons of Horus (Imseti, Hapi, Duamutef, and Kebehsenuef) were appointed by their father to guard the four cardinal points and the viscera and heart of Osiris.

"truth": In Egyptian representations of the Judgment of the Dead, an important scene is that of *psychostasia*, the weighing of the dead person's soul. Anubis or Horus put the heart of the deceased into one of the pans of the scale, Maat (the goddess of truth and justice), or her symbol—the ostrich feather (the ideogram of her name)—in the other.

IX "Woman from Chianciano" (p. 34)

She is a limestone cinerary statue, 0.9 meters high, from the territory of Chiusi, and dates from c. 450 BC; in the Museo Archeologico, Florence. Her head functions as a lid. Found inside her, along with a gold fibula, was an Attic *oinochoe* in the shape of a woman's head.

X "Vortex" (p. 36)

The beast sits at the center of the lid of a bronze situla in the Villa Giulia, Rome. The other figures stand on the lid and shoulders of the situla, which is 32 cm high, dates from 720–700 BC, and comes from a tomb in the cemetery of Olmo Bello, at the foot of Mount Bisenzio. Bisenzio, on the western shore of Lake Bolsena, was inhabited from the Iron Age through the Middle Ages. In Roman times it was called Visentium.

XI "Porta all'Arco, Volterra" (p. 37)

Velathri is the Etruscan name of modern Volterra (Roman Volaterrae).

"signs and portents, the earth and sky": To read these signs and interpret the will of the gods, one had to have a proper orientation. And that orientation had to reflect the divine one, the *templum caeleste*, the vault of the heavens in which Tinia and the other gods dwelled. Enthroned in the North, Tinia faced the South. To his left, in the East, the constellations rose; and this part, the *pars sinistra* or *familiaris*, was considered of good omen. To his right, in the West, where the constellations set, was the *pars dextra* or *hostilis*—a region of ill omen. Representing the heavens as a circle, the Etruscan diviner (be he fulguriator, haruspex, or augur) drew a line bisecting the circle from north to south, which was called the *cardo*; a second bisecting line, running east-west, was the *decumanus*. Tinia had three dwellings in the northeastern quadrant so formed, and thus this quadrant was most auspicious. The fifth-century AD author Martianus Capellus, in his work *De Nuptiis Philologiae et Mercurii*, describes the Etruscan method of quartering and further quartering the circle into sixteen dwellings for their various gods. In the Northeast Capella locates the celestial gods, in the Southeast and Southwest the gods of the earth and of nature, in the Northwest the infernal deities. To take and read the signs, the diviner stationed himself at the intersection of *cardo* and *decumanus* and faced south as Tinia did. Porta all'Arco is Volterra's southern gate; its three heads look southward.

"the god's command": According to the *Libri Rituales*, a city had to be founded and laid out in a prescribed manner. The city founded in accordance with Etruscan *rite* was a reflection of the *templum caeleste* as described above.

Groma: An instrument used for surveying land; had the word come into Latin directly from Greek, without Etruscan intermediation, its form would have been *gnoma*.

Capaneus: One of the seven against Thebes. In Volterra's Museo Guarnacci, there is a late third-century BC alabaster urn with a relief depicting the death of Capaneus. The Etruscan sculptor used the Porta all'Arco as his model for one of the Theban gates.

Panchina: A yellow or brown sandstone, a kind of tufa which may contain marine substances. *Peperino*: A light, porous, small-grained volcanic tufa formed of sand, cinders, etc. The dark gray variety usually comes from the Alban hills. *Travertino*: Travertine, crystalline calcium carbonate formed by deposition from spring waters.

"the coin of the realm": Larger coins have the dolphin, smaller coins have a club or crescent in its place. The Janus-head is the arms of Volterra.

XII *"From Vetulonia"* (p. 40)

These mute creatures are of bronze, date from 675–600 BC, and reside in the Museo Archeologico, Florence. They were found near the Circle (or Tomb) of the Costiaccia Bambagini, Vetulonia.

"axeheads": The invention of the *fascis*—a bundle of rods sheathing an axe—was assigned by Silius Italicus (*Punica*, VIII, 483ff.) to Vetulonia. Strangely enough, Vetulonia is the only place that has supplied an actual specimen. The small votive model, of bronze, found by Falchi in 1898, is in the Museo Archeologico, Florence.

Pars Sinistra (Familiaris)

I *"The Mummy Speaks"* (p. 45)

The language of the Etruscans, while legible, is yet to be properly deciphered. The "Book of the Mummy," a *liber linteus*—the only preserved example of a manuscript book on linen cloth, was originally a *volumen* (roll) cut into strips and used for mummy wrappings. Still extant in the National Museum of Zagreb (Agram is the German name of the city), are about twelve columns, written from right to left in red and black ink.

The Etruscan verses quoted in the poem are the first six lines of Column VII. The source for the transcription is M. Runes's *Der etruskische Text der Agramer Mumienbinden* (Göttingen, 1935). I have replaced theta's with th's. For several wildly divergent renditions of these same six lines see James Wellard's *The Search for the Etruscans* (New York: Saturday Review Press, 1973), pp. 186–191.

II "God's Breath" (p. 48)

Even Freud dreamt about these quizzical objects. For his dream about the "breakfast-ship," see *The Interpretation of Dreams*, translated and edited by James Strachey (1965, New York: Discus/Avon, [8th printing], 1971) pp. 500–506.

Various examples of heavy-walled, black *bucchero focolari* can be seen in Chiusi (Museo Nazionale Etrusco), Copenhagen (Ny Carlsberg Glyptotek), New York (Metropolitan Museum of Art), and Rome (Villa Giulia), among other places.

III "La Defunta" (p. 50)

Tomba del Barone: The Tomb of the Baron at Tarquinia was discovered in 1827 by Barone di Stackelberg (from whom it takes its name) and Chevalier Kestner; it dates from about 500 BC (perhaps somewhat earlier).

Pallium (pl. *pallia*): A large rectangular cloak or mantle.

The last stanza echoes the stanza of Goethe's *Erlkönig* which begins, "*Willst, feiner Knabe, du mit mir gehn?*"

IV "Hand to Hand" (p. 52)

"Ivory, brittle . . .": From Praeneste (Palestrina), Barberini Tomb, 670–650 BC, in the Villa Giulia, Rome.

"Attached to . . .": From Vulci, VI–V century BC, in the Villa Giulia, Rome.

"Can you still see . . .": Two pairs from

Vulci, in the Villa Giulia, Rome.

"Two rows of golden . . .": From Vulci, in the Museo Gregoriano Etrusco, Vatican.

Patera: a libation bowl, a broad flat dish with an umbo in the center.

V *"The Stonecutter at Norchia" (p. 54)*

The chief rupestral necropoli, the cemeteries of the cliff-tomb cities, along the Marta and its tributaries are Bieda, Castel d'Asso, Norchia, San Giovenale, and San Giuliano. Norchia's necropolis is especially renowned for its "temple" tombs, which have sculptured pediments and porticoed facades.

VI *"Fabric of Ceremony" (p. 57)*

The object under scrutiny is a low relief on one side of a small urn in the form of a temple, of which only the upper part remains. It is in Chiusi's Museo Nazionale Etrusco, dates from the fourth century BC, and is of *pietra fetida*. *Pietra fetida*, or fetid limestone, is the local limestone that comes from the region of Chianciano. It is a kind of tufa formed by and imbued with sulfurous waters. It is called "fetid" because of the odor of sulfur or garlic which emanates from it when it is cut and removed from the quarry.

VII *"Hut Urn" (p. 58)*

I do not have any particular one in mind. The seven found at Tarquinia are dated as Early Villanovan I. These cinerary urns imitate conical hut dwellings of wicker-work and are indeed ancient. Others have been found in the Alban hills, some beneath strata of *peperino*, and may contain the ashes of the inhabitants of Alba Longa. For additional descriptions of tumulus tombs see "Lucien's Ploughman 1848" and "La Banditaccia, 1979."

VIII *"Gorgoneion" (p. 59)*

The fifth-century BC bronze *"lampadario di Cortona"* presently hangs in the Museo dell'Accademia Etrusca di Cortona. Dennis believed it was a *lychnus*, a sacrificial lamp that was hung from the ceilings of palaces or temples, or as have been found suspended in Etruscan sepulchres. It was found, not in a tomb, but in a ditch, not far below the surface of the soil, in 1840, at a place called La Fratta, at the foot of Mount Cortona, on the road to Montepulciano. A Signor Tommasi is said to have paid the peasants who found it $700 for their find. On his death, his wife presented the lamp to the Accademia Etrusca.

The Accademia Etrusca at Cortona was founded in 1726; its presiding officer is given the title of *lucumo*.

Euryale: Of the three Gorgons, Euryale ("wide-leaping"), Sthenno (or Sthenusa, the "mighty one"), and Medusa ("queen"), only the last was mortal. In some accounts, Athena herself (who bears the gorgoneion òn her shield or on the aegis) is said to have killed the Gorgon in the battle with the Giants.

Tibia: The double pipes. Athena was credited with the invention of the flute (Greek *aulos*, Latin *tibia*). In doing so, according to Pindar, she mimicked the wild lamentations and the hissing of the snake-infested .hair of the other Gorgons at the time of Medusa's death.

IX "*Calchas, Haruspex*" (p. 61)

The speaker of this poem is a composite resulting from the metamorphosis of two objects of bronze, both of which reside in the same case in the Museo Gregoriano Etrusco in the Vatican. The first of these is a small bronze statuette (9 cm high), dating from about 350 BC. The second is a bronze mirror from Vulci, named for its inscription (which reads from left to right) "Calchas"; it dates from about 460 BC.

The art of *haruspicina* in first-century BC Rome referred to the whole science of divination. Earlier, however, it pertained only to the examination of animal entrails, and particularly to the examination of livers from sacrificial animals. In the Roman method of examining entrails, they remained in the animal's body. The Etruscan *haruspex*, or to use their own word, *netśvis*, removed the liver from the victim's body.

"the Veiled, the Nameless Ones": The *Dii Involuti*; see note to "The Warning."

"I sanctified the grove": Any area on earth, providing it could be enclosed, could be sanctified, if properly oriented and subdivided. See note to "Porta all'Arco, Volterra."

"the gland's sixteen zones": The liver of the victim was also seen as a *templum* (cf. note to "Porta all'Arco"). A second-century BC bronze model of a ·

sheep's liver, found near Piacenza in 1877, was probably used in instructing haruspices. Around the rim of its upper surface are sixteen compartments, in each of which is incised a name, probably of the various Etruscan gods and goddesses.

"my left foot rests . . .": Evidently the ritualistic stance of the *netśvis*. It is similarly represented on the so-called "Tarchon Mirror" from Tuscania (Toscanella). The mirror dates from the third century BC and would seem to depict Pavatarchies (perhaps an Etruscan form of Tages) instructing Tarchunos (Tarchon) in liver scrutiny.

Temple of Nortia, doctrine of the *saecula*: Nortia was believed to be a goddess analogous to the Roman Fortuna. Her temple, supposed to be at Volsinii, has never been found. According to Livy, ceremonies were held at the close of each year at Nortia's Temple, at which time a "year-nail" was driven into its wall, making that wall a national calendar for Etruria. According to the *Libri Fatales,* different peoples had an existence of predetermined duration, as assigned by Fate. The *Nomen Etruscum* was assigned eight, or by another tradition ten, *saecula.* The precise length of a *saeculum* was not fixed; it began with the end of the preceding one and extended until the death of the last of all those who had been alive at its inception.

Rasenna or *Rásna* was the name the Etruscans called themselves. The Romans called them *Tusci* or *Etrusci*; the Greeks called them *Tyrrhenians* or *Tyrsenians.* Arnobius, a Christian writer of the fourth century AD, called them *genetrix et mater superstitionis.*

X "Final Questions" (p. 64)

The speaker of this poem, who may well be Iphegenia, appears on two of the "Campana Slabs," which are in the Louvre, Paris. The slabs (*pinakes*) are of terracotta; before applying paint to them, the artist first coated them with a thin layer of plaster, into which he traced the figures' broad outlines. They are named for the Marchese G. P. Campana, their first owner; come from a tomb opened at Cerveteri in 1856, and date from 530–520 BC.

XI "La Banditaccia, 1979" (p. 66)

Cerveteri (Caere Vetus) is the modern Italian name of the

city known to the Romans as Caere. The word "cere-
mony" may possibly be related to the name of the city.
To the Greeks the city was known as Agylla; the Etrus-
cans called is Cisra, Kysry, or Xaire.

"shepherds their flocks": In Dennis's day
the *pecoraio* still marched at the head of his flock, calling
the sheep to follow him. In more remote times, not only
sheep but also swine, oxen, and goats in Italy and on
Corsica, according to Polybius, followed the sound of
their herdsman's trumpet.

"the Zone": The archaeological zone or
zona recinto. Not all the tombs described here are within
it, but can be reached, with the help of a local guide, off
the road between the town and the necropolis.

La grotta bella, also called *la tomba dei rilievi*,
belonged to the Mantuna family, effigies of some of
whom appear in stucco on the tomb's pilasters.

XII   "Degli Sposi" (p. 69)

Except to distinguish it from the similar but overly re-
stored example in the Louvre, the terracotta "Sarcopha-
gus of the Married Couple" in the Villa Giulia, Rome,
needs little commentary. It comes from Caere (Cerve-
teri), dates from the second half of the sixth century BC,
and was reconstructed from about 400 fragments.

N

Etruscan

Things

S